The Adventures of Gnome on the go

A Family Travel Tradition

Justina Davis &
Alexa Menard

The Adventures of Gnome on the Go

Printed in the USA by JWG Publishing House

DEDICATION

"To Peyton, Tripp, and Schyler my greatest joys.
Never stop chasing your dreams, and always
believe in your ability to achieve them. You
inspire me every day to be the best mom I can
be and to follow my own dreams."
– Justina Davis

"To my children who inspire me and fill my
heart every day, I love you unconditionally.
To my parents who showed me hard work,
determination, support and love."
– Alexa Menard

MISSION & VISION

Our mission is to foster a sense of community
and adventure by bringing joy and inclusivity
to people of all backgrounds and ages through
unique and engaging travel experiences with
Gnome On The Go.

In a little gnome village tucked away between rolling hills and babbling brooks lived two extraordinary gnomes named Gracie and Gavin. They were known far and wide as the "Gnomies".

Gracie with her pink polka dot hat and Gavin with his spiffy blue suspenders loved new adventures and making friends wherever they went.

8

One sunny morning, Gracie and Gavin discovered a magical camera and a collection of flags. The flags sparkled with possibilities and each flag represented a new place to explore and visit. They knew they would see different states, countries, and sporting events.

The gnomes knew they were going on a great adventure. So, they put on their backpacks and with a heart full of dreams set off on their quest to explore.

Gracie and Gavin began their adventure in New York City, they could not believe how big the skyscrapers were and how many yellow cars there were. Of course, those yellow cars were taxicabs, something they had never seen before.

They took selfies with the pigeons holding their NY flag which would be the first flag proudly added to their growing collection.

Next on their big adventure was the Grand Canyon in Arizona. They headed to the Grand Canyon and Gracie and Gavin could not believe the breathtaking views of the red rocks and the wide canyons. The canyons are believed to be 5 million years old and 277 miles long.

Grand Canyon

They stopped to take a picture so they could share with all their friends the different places they were exploring, but they were careful not to go too close to the canyon's edge.

From there, Gracie and Gavin traveled to the sunny beaches of Florida. They had a great time building sandcastles and sea creatures and swimming with the dolphins.

They put their Florida flag at the top of the sandcastle. They giggled as they took selfies while the waves crashed on their feet.

Gracie and Gavin continued their adventures to Europe...

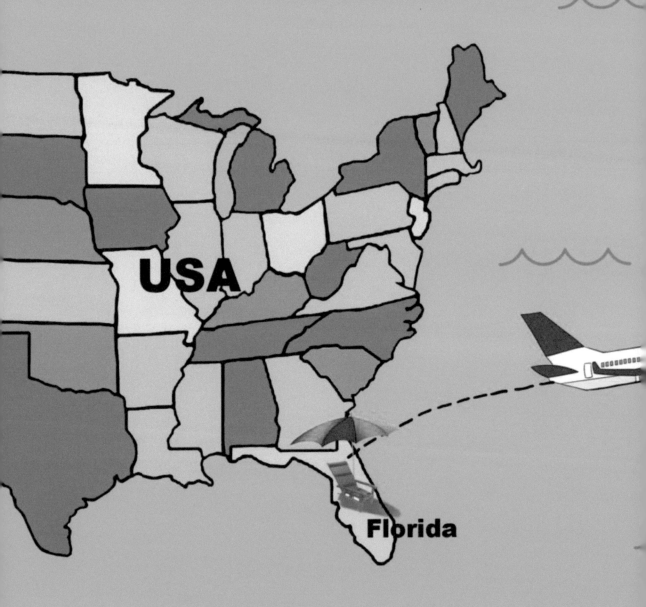

EUROPE

Paris

18

Gracie and Gavin strolled down the historic streets of Paris, dancing beneath the Eiffel Towel and eating croissants with their new friends.

Their gnome sized camera clicked away preserving the memories of their European adventure. The flag with Paris on it would be their first they collected from exploring Europe.

PARIS

Gracie and Gavin posted pictures of their adventures so all the gnomes in the gnome village could see where they've been and connect through their shared experiences while they encourage others to travel, explore and follow their dreams.

They continued their journey visiting the colosseum in Rome and the windmills in the Netherlands.

HOLLAND

Each destination brought new friendships, learning about new cultures, and trying new food. Their flag collection was growing, and they were very excited about this. In each new country they continued to learn about that country's traditions.

| HOLLAND | 2 |
| ARGENTINA | 1 |

Gracie and Gavin also wanted to experience vibrant cultures, attend sporting events and cheering on their favorite teams.

They went to a football game which is known in the USA as soccer and there they saw Holland play against Argentina. They loved exchanging stories of their adventures with new friends they would meet along the way.

As the Gnomies traveled, they spread the message of adventure, friendship and following one's dreams. Their gnome-sized camera captured moments of laughter, kindness, and shared joy, leaving a trail of inspiration for the gnomes and humans alike. It was important to Gracie and Gavin to be very inclusive and make others feel welcome.

Eventually Gracie and Gavin returned to their gnome village, their backpacks filled with flags, memories and friendships made around the world.

They were excited to display their flags so everyone could see where they traveled to and how they connected with other gnomes and people all over the world.

They knew they would continue to travel in life and always collect flags as a reminder of their adventures.

29

And so, the legend of Gracie and Gavin, the Gnomies who traveled the world, became an inspiration, encouraging gnomes of all ages to dream BIG, explore, create friendships, and embark on their own grand adventure.

They would daydream of their next adventure and different places that they planned to travel to, excited to make new friends and learn

The End

TRAVEL JOURNAL

Let's get going...

Travel Destination

Dates of travel

What we saw

What we did

Who we traveled with

What flags did you collect while on your adventure?

What did I like most about the trip?

What did I like least about the trip?

What landmarks did you visit?

What are the names of friends you made on your adventure?

How long was your trip?

Where do you want to explore next?

TRAVEL JOURNAL

TRAVEL JOURNAL

TRAVEL JOURNAL

47205237R00020